HEADS U

Here Comes College

By Jim Frank Mullen M Ed

Weasel Monkeys LLC

"Every 8th grade student should read this book."

Mrs. Catherine Westbury M Ed NBCT
Missouri School Counselor of the Year 2010
Peabody Energy Leader in Education 2013

10% of profits are dedicated to distributing
<u>Heads Up 8th Grader!</u> to struggling students.

Dear Parents & Educators,

From the first day of kindergarten children have been told about the importance of learning.

Learning is important.

But schools do not tell students the whole story.

<u>Heads Up 8th Grader!</u> shines a light on the dark side of education…GPA, ACT, ranking, college acceptance and…MONEY.

This book is designed to be read two weeks before entering the 8th grade but could benefit students at any grade level.

Practical unique "how to" strategies are provided to improve grades and test scores.

It also creates the structure, vocabulary, and time frames that spark crucial discussions about high school and college.

Ideally, students will be enlightened and motivated by understanding how the K-12 education system affects college and the rest of their lives.

Twenty years of teaching middle school has led me to create this book. Eighth graders need to know the truth, they need to look up.

Heads Up 8th Grader!

~Jim Frank Mullen

STUDENTS...

WHY...

Imagine a place;

A wondrous place, away from your

parents...

a place where hundreds or even

thousands of 18 to 22 years olds

live, hang out, and learn.

A 4 year adventure!

COLLEGE!

Raise your hand if you <u>PLAN</u> to go to college.

Do you know how much college costs?

Going to college IS fun

PAYING for it is not.

This is important...to YOU...hang in there...

There are over 6,000 Higher Education institutions in America.

There are many different kinds.

But mostly it looks like this...

1. <u>JUNIOR COLLEGE</u>
- 2 year school
- Financially assisted by the State
- Less expensive than 4 year schools
- You can earn credits or an "Associate's Degree" which will transfer to a 4 year school
- No Dorms or on campus housing
- Limited college life, not the move away from home "college experience"

2. <u>STATE COLLEGES & UNIVERSITIES</u>

- 4 year schools
- Financially assisted by the State
- Usually less expensive than Private Schools
- Better reputation than Jr. Colleges
- Dorms & on campus housing
- Traditional college experience

3. <u>PRIVATE COLLEGES & UNIVERSITIES</u>

- 4 year schools
- Run by private individuals or organizations
- Better reputation (sometimes) than State Schools
- Dorms & on campus housing
- Traditional college experience

Let's pick on a STATE SCHOOL, just for fun...

The University of Missouri at Columbia,

MIZZOU. 🐾

🐾 MIZ! ZOU!

GREAT SCHOOL- REALLY FUN-

GREAT REPUTATION.

Tuition for one semester is about $9,000.

That's $18,000 per year.

Add housing, food, books, etc...

Easily $25,000 per year (rounding).  WHAT?!?

I DIDN'T KNOW

Times 4 years = $100,000. IT COST ...

THAT MUCH

And that is a state school. Most PRIVATE

schools cost more.

You say you plan to go to college...

Raise your hand if you have a PLAN to PAY for college.

It's time to have a HEADS UP!

It's time to look ahead and understand the

HIGH SCHOOL ~ MONEY ~ COLLEGE
CONNECTION.

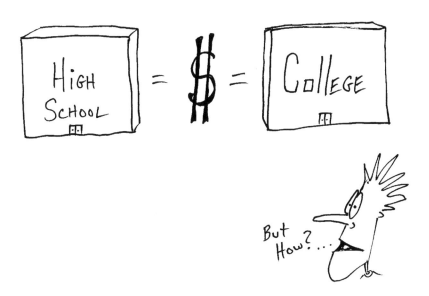

The more you understand how the system
WORKS...

the more you can WORK THE SYSTEM!

Here's the trick...

You have to start in 8th Grade because everything counts starting the first day of 9th grade.

You don't want to try to figure this stuff out while it's counting against you.

Your first quarter 9th grade GPA is as important as your last quarter 12th grade GPA.

Understanding the system and how to work it will not only help you for college but will also give you tremendous

<u>LEVERAGE NOW</u>

LEVERAGE? I LIKE THE... SOUND OF THAT.

against your parents, teachers, & time.

ARE YOU IN?

What does it take to get into and pay for college?

...GRADES!

What are the Top 3 things colleges are looking for?

...umm

Top 3 things

1. G.P.A.

2. A.C.T.

3. The **X**tra Factor

G.P.A.

➤ Do you know what GPA stands for?

YES...

➤ Do you know how your GPA is CALCULATED?

..GRADES ?

➤ Do you know what a CUMULATIVE GPA is?

...umm

➤ Do you know what high school GPA RANKING is?

...NO.

➤ Do you have a 4.0 GPA?

A.C.T.

➤ Do you know what the ACT is?

➤ Do you know what kind of QUESTIONS are on the test?

➤ Do you know how IMPORTANT your ACT score is?

I'M ONLY ... 14.

➤ Have you started PRACTICING the ACT yet?

The **X**tra Factor

➤ *Do you play any sports?*

➤ *Were you in the play?*

XTRA STUFF...

➤ *Stuco, Chess Club, Volunteering?*

➤ ***ANYTHING XTRA ?!?!?!***

➤ *Have you posted anything DUMB on Facebook, Snapchat, Instagram...etc? (It has kept kids out of college).*

NO....

➤ *Do you have a polished presentation of your documented school participation?*

HOW...

I'M
... READY!

G.P.A.

GPA stands for GRADE POINT AVERAGE.
When you get a grade on your report card,
each grade is worth so many points...

A = 4

B = 3

C = 2

D = 1

F = 0

If you have 7 classes and receive an "A" in all 7 classes it would look like this...

Math = A

LA   = A

Gym = A

SS = A

Art = A

Music = A

Science = A

THIS is
HOW THEY
JUDGE WHAT
...WE KNOW?

Each "A" is worth 4 points X's 7 classes...

4 X 7 = 28 points.

28 divided by the 7 classes equals your GPA

or

28 / 7 = 4.0 GPA

All "B's" would look like this...

Math = B

LA   = B

Gym = B

SS = B

Art = B

Music = B

Science = B

B's ARE ...WORTH 3 ?

Each "B" is worth 3 points X's 7 classes...

3 X 7 = 21 points.

21 divided by the 7 classes equals your GPA

or

21 / 7 = 3.0 GPA

SERIOUSLY...

And so on and so forth.

School THEN takes your GPA's from 9th, 10th, 11th, & 12th grade and averages them to come up with your CUMULATIVE GPA.

9th = 3·0   3·0

10th = 3·5   3·5

11th= 2·5   2·5

12th = 4·0   +4·0
                       ____

                        13

THAT'S THE BEST THEY COULD ∴ COME UP WITH?

13 / 4 years = 3·25 CUMULATIVE GPA

THEN...

Schools take all the kids in your graduating class and RANKS them in order from highest CUMULATIVE GPA to lowest.

4.0 GPA

THAT'S ... JUST WRONG.

0.0 GPA

This is your

HIGH SCHOOL RANKING

... THE TOP...DUH.

Do you think colleges want the kids at the TOP or the bottom of the RANKING?

SO...

You PLAN to go to college...

I'M NOT ..A 4.0 STUDENT.

WHY DON'T YOU HAVE A 4.0 GPA?

No really...

WHY DON'T YOU HAVE A 4·0 GPA?

OK...

__WHY__ IS SCHOOL LESS THAN WONDERFUL?

Why do you sit in desks so much?

Why are there so many kids in class?

Why does it start so early?

Why don't you have more free time?

Longer lunches, better technology, etc?!?!?

... I'VE NEVER THOUGHT OF "WHY"

To answer that, you have to answer this...

WHY ARE YOU IN SCHOOL IN THE FIRST PLACE?

— WHAT?

Why are you in school?

...TO LEARN!

Nope.

TO PREPARE US FOR ...LIFE.

Nope.

SO WE ...CAN GET A JOB.

Nope.

...TELL ME!

About 100 years ago this country worked little kids in FACTORIES.

Most of you reading this would be working 10-14 hours a day.

The adults that worked in those factories got together and said "these kids are taking our jobs, get them out of here or we won't work at all." . . .

The country passed a law saying kids couldn't work until age 16.

What did they do with all those kids that were working in the factories?

Right.

They made a law that said you HAVE to go to school...

TO KEEP YOU OUT OF THE WORK FORCE.

And it was the time of the INDUSTRIAL REVOLUTION so they modeled schools after assembly line factories.

They broke down learning into ELEMENTS (the smallest parts)...reading, writing, arithmetic... created a learning factory and sent you down the assembly line.

Now that it is the 21st Century, why are you still in a SCHOOL FACTORY?

Why not have...

- Smaller classes
- The latest technology
- On-line learning
- Build knowledge through experience & reflecting
- Work closely with real businesses & community

THAT WOULD COST TOO MUCH.

YES. School seems less than wonderful because it is built on the least expensive model to educate large amounts of children.

So...
WHAT DOES
THAT MEAN
TO ME?

It means you are legally stuck in the system and you only have 4 options to deal with it.

4 OPTIONS

1. <u>REBEL</u>...

Colleges do NOT give $ to rebels.

2. <u>CHANGE THE SYSTEM</u>...

It would be almost impossible to change the system as a student. But if that is your thing, go for it, the world needs changers.

3. <u>"JUST GETTIN' BY"</u>

Do just enough to keep parents & teachers off your back. Again...no $ HEY...

4. <u>WORK THE SYSTEM</u> = $$$

To WORK THE SYSTEM

you have to first understand...

<u>10-14-18</u>

<u>10</u>

4 years ago you were a little kid.

<u>14</u>

You are right in the middle.

You can look back and act like a kid,

or have a <u>HEADS UP</u> &

be treated like a young adult.

<u>18</u>

4 years from now you will be a legal adult.

Next...

It is important to understand school is divided into 2 parts

Learning VS· Points

Learning is important...

But...

POINTS = GPA

GPA = $$$$

YOU MUST GET ALL THE POINTS

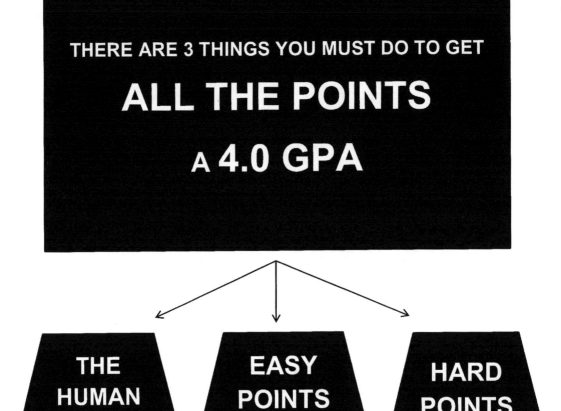

The Human Factor

BE COOL TO YOUR TEACHERS.

You have to have them on your side.

Say HI, TALK to them, say THANK YOU.

Treat them like they are real people.

The majority of grading is subjective, directly controlled by teachers.

Working the system will not work without the Human Factor.

Easy Points

- *EASY POINTS are any points EASY to get...word searches, coloring, crosswords, etc.*
- *We all HATE doing this mindless busy work so much that we don't do it.*
- *Not doing easy points results in zero's.*
- *"O's" CRUSH GPA's.*
- *NEVER MISS ANOTHER EASY POINT!*

HARD POINTS

```
         TESTS              PROJECTS
```

TESTS

At the _beginning_ of each new unit, the first day _after_ a big test...

ASK THE TEACHER WHAT CHAPTERS,
READING ASSIGNMENTS,
AND ANY OTHER MATERIAL
ARE GOING TO BE ON THE _REALLY..._
NEXT TEST.

Once you know EXACTLY
which chapters are going to be covered on
THE NEXT TEST...

GO HOME AND READ ALL

OF IT THE FIRST

NIGHT

...Noooo!

ARE
YOU
...NUTS?

I KNOW,
YOU THINK I'M CRAZY
STICK WITH ME
FOR JUSTA MINUTE...

*I know this sounds like work &
goody goody stuff.*

IT'S NOT.
IT'S SERIOUS.
IT WORKS!
READ IT ALL.
TRUST ME.
TRY IT.
AT LEAST ONCE- TRY IT.

TENS OF THOUSANDS OF DOLLARS
ARE ON THE LINE!

Once you pre-read all the material on the first
night before the new unit,
go back to class the next day and the teacher
will start talking about the material.

YOU have just read it.
Your brain HEARS what you just read and
automatically tries to get a better
understanding of the subject.
You will actually have some
questions about the reading.
Ask your questions!

It's
Too
EASY
...

You will sit there and think-
Why is the teacher going on and on about this
stuff? It's all right there in the book.
I JUST READ IT.

What do "*Just Gettin' By*" students do?
They don't read it.

So when the teacher starts talking about new information
they don't know what the teacher's talking about.
Their brains do not tune in.

To them it sounds like Charlie Brown's teacher-
"waa waa, waa wa waa wa."

So
TRUE...

In fact, most of their time is spent trying to avoid eye contact with the teacher
because they don't want to get called on
BECAUSE THEY DIDN'T READ IT.

Now the teacher hands out boring
<u>WORKSHEETS</u>·

YOU KNOW WHERE THE ANSWERS ARE
LOCATED IN THE BOOK
BECAUSE YOU ALREADY READ IT!

"JUST GETTIN' BY" STUDENTS
either copy their friends work or
HUNT AND PECK at their worksheets.
...HA! TRUE AGAIN.
They HUNT through the reading material, not
reading it,
PECKING for something that
LOOKS like what is on the worksheet.

When they find it, without reading it, they
write it down,
THIS TAKES LONGER
&
GETS LESS POINTS
MORE TIME...

HAVING READ IT-
YOU CAN DO THE WORKHEET IN MOMENTS.
GIVING YOU MORE SOCIAL TIME!

NOW IT'S TEST TIME

At least 3 Days before the test you need to ASK...

- How many questions are on the test?
- What is the format of the test?
- How many multiple choice questions are there?
- How many matching?
- How many fill in the blank, etc·?
- What kind of information will be covered by which format?
- ASK if specific charts, maps, big information, etc· will be on the test·

REAlly

THE MORE INFORMATION YOU CAN GET OUT OF YOUR TEACHER, THE EASIER STUDYING BECOMES!

IT DOES ...MAKE SENSE

You also need to ask your teacher for a

STUDY GUIDE!

Think about it...

What do you think MOST study guides are made out of?

MOST STUDY GUIDES ARE MADE OUT OF THE ACTUAL TEST!

MAYBE I SHOULD LOOK AT MY STUDY GUIDE . . .

Most teachers make the test on a WORD document FIRST.

Then they cut and paste and change it up a bit to create the study guide-

but IT IS THE TEST- JUST REARRANGED!

They do this because it is the easiest way for them to do it.

I have spent 20 years behind the desk-

I AM NOT KIDDING!

After you take the first test
with a new teacher...

It is important to be aware of how your teacher used her test to MAKE her study guide.

ASK for your test back when she is finished grading it. COMPARE the old study guide to the test. Figure out how she "changed" her test into the study guide. Learn to recognize what your next test will look like based on your old study guide.

THEN...

COMPARE the old test to the book. How many vocab words were on the test? How many questions were made from the chapter summary? Try to figure out where her TEST QUESTIONS CAME FROM! Teachers tend to follow the same pattern when creating their test. Once you figure out how your teacher creates her tests, the rest of her test should be totally easy!

<u>This skill will help you</u>
<u>all the way through college.</u>

If you do poorly on a test,

TALK to your teacher, ASK to retake the test.

PROJECTS

Projects include papers, posters, computer & oral presentations, and/or anything that is not regular homework, tests, or easy points.

The Goal of THE PROJECT

- GET 100% OF THE POINTS.
- QUICKLY & EFFECTIVLY.

TO ACHIEVE THE GOAL
YOU MUST HAVE A <u>SCORING GUIDE</u>.

<u>Make your teacher give you one if you have to!</u>

The scoring guide NEEDS to break down the total amount of points into smaller pieces, explaining how to achieve 100% of the points. Example...

- 5 points for title
- 10 points for introduction paragraph
- 60 points for body
- 25 points for closing

Once you get your scoring guide, highlight

 -with a highlighter-

...REALLY?

EXACTLY what the teacher requires for each set of points.

KNOW WHAT IS REQUIRED
FOR EACH SET OF POINTS
BEFORE YOU START

Real Life Story...

The last 5 minutes before school let out for spring break my 8th grade son's teacher said, "Over Spring Break I want you to look up 10 astronomers throughout history and put them in chronological order, have a good Spring Break."

My son tells us this, in the van, on the way to the beach.

I say "Where is the scoring guide?"

He says "We didn't get one."

Now my wife is involved.

We have no idea if this is a big, medium, or small project.

This instantly became the NIGHTMARE PROJECT.

My son announces he will do it when we get home, which is the night before we all return to school. My wife is already researching on her phone.

The three of us "discussed" when and how to do his project, several times...

Finally, they took a day off from the beach and created an AMAZING poster board project, complete with a painted star background, planets, photo print outs, and paragraphs written about each astronomer. My wife was thrilled, my son was not.

He returned to school on the following Monday with his project and presented it to the teacher. The teacher said "Oh, I did ask you guys to do that didn't I, that wasn't for a grade you know, but it looks nice."

My son learned two lessons that spring break, the chronological order of major astronomers throughout history and ...

GET A SCORING GUIDE!

Real Life Story...

I checked on my son doing his homework. I opened the door and he was flopping around on his desk like a fish out of water. "What are you doing?" I asked. "I have to write a poem about myself" he grumbled. "So what's wrong?" I asked. "I don't know what to write. I don't know what the teacher wants. I called my friends and they aren't sure either." "How long have you been trying to do this?" I asked. "An hour!" he snapped. "How long did the teacher give you in class?" I asked. "A half an hour on Thursday and Friday" he said. "So you have 2 hours on this project so far. Where is your scoring guide?" I asked. "I KNOW what to do, we have to write a poem ABOUT OURSELVES!" he said with attitude, flopping around his desk some more.

I made him dig a crumpled scoring guide out of his back pack. He had never even looked at it.

I got out a highlighter and sat down with him. He was mad and didn't want to take the time to go through it.

First, we had to get through a bunch of teacher talk on the scoring guide...bla bla bla...about poetry and its importance.

Next, I highlighted 10 points for a proper heading and title, which he did not have on his paper.

Then, I highlighted 80 points for the poem, and finally, 10 points for the conclusion.

The best part was the teacher had written the first words of the 8 lines of the poem ON THE SCORING GUIDE and just wanted students to finish the lines using personal information- AND THAT WAS IT. Then write a couple of lines describing the poem.

My son looked at me in disbelief, he couldn't believe that's all there was to the assignment.

He was completely finished in less than 15 minutes.

Hmm...
Highlighter.

HIGHLIGHT
YOUR SCORING GUIDE
BEFORE YOU START!

Once you have a scoring guide, and you know
exactly what is required for each set of points,
NO MATTER HOW BIG THE ASSIGNMENT IS...

GO HOME AND DO YOUR

...NOOOO!

ENTIRE

PROJECT

THE FIRST NIGHT IT

IS ASSIGNED!

ARE YOU ...NUTS?

I KNOW,
YOU THINK I'M CRAZY
STICK WITH ME
FOR JUSTA MINUTE...

As kids,

we all learn that if we finish our work early,

"old people"

JUST GIVE US MORE WORK!

So, we learn to put our assignments off
till the very last minute to avoid getting more
work.

NOT ANY MORE!

Finish the assignment the FIRST DAY and make
the rest of the "in class" work time YOURS.

YOU ARE NOW OLD ENOUGH,

YOU HAVE TO TRAIN YOUR TEACHERS
TO GIVE YOU THE TIME!

(Another reason to be cool to your teachers.)

Project Summary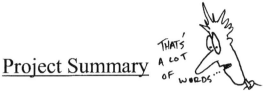

1. GO HOME AND FINISH THE PROJECT THE FIRST DAY IT IS ASSIGNED. If you have a partner, tell them to come over that night or you are doing it without them.

2. The NEXT day, bring the completed assignment into the teacher. YES, YOUR TEACHERS AND FRIENDS WILL FREAK, DO IT ANYWAY, THEY GET USED TO IT QUICKLY.

3. Show the teacher your highlighted score guide and where you have checked off each section.

4. Ask the teacher to please look over the project and let you know if there is anything you need to improve. ASK! IF THERE ARE ANY missing points that you can fix. ASK- IS IT 100%. Think about it, it took you a couple hours to get most of the points, but once your teacher tells you what to correct, you can correct them in moments to get ALL the points.

5. Go home and redo, add, fix, do whatever the teacher said to do and bring it back the NEXT day.

6. MAKE SURE YOU HAVE YOUR 100%. GET ALL THE POINTS! It makes a difference when you average this grade with your test grades!

7. Then, if there is any "in class" work time for the project (the one you just completed the first day), QUIETLY get some other school work out and start to do it. Teachers see everything, if she lets it go, you are free and clear. If not, QUIETLY & PRIVATELY ask the teacher, "Do you mind if I please work on this other school work that I have, since I have 100% on my project? This other work is due soon and I am REALLY anxious to get it done, please? I promise I will not disrupt your class."

8. At this point, especially since you have engaged the HUMAN FACTOR (treated your teacher cool) since the beginning of the school year, **MOST TEACHERS WILL GIVE YOU THE TIME.**

9. YOU WILL BE AMAZED AT THE AMOUNT OF "IN CLASS" TIME YOU CAN CREATE FOR YOURSELF BY FINISHING YOUR PROJECT THE FIRST DAY! THIS EXTRA TIME IS WHEN YOU GET AHEAD ON ALL YOUR WORK AND **FREE UP EVEN MORE OF YOUR EVENINGS!**

I'M SERIOUS, IT WORKS!

Real Life Story...

When I was in college I would go to class and they would assign a paper due the next week. I had several classes, so I had several papers due each week.

Before I had a HEADS UP! the nightmare looked like this...
I always put my papers off until the very last moment. On the night before each paper was due I would go home worrying about my paper, take a nap, eat some dinner- while worrying-, and then go out to a party or go dancing. I would tell myself that I would write the paper AFTER I went out for the night.

More than once I fell asleep on my computer key board at 2am. I finished a lot of papers in the early morning light the day they were due. I skipped classes because I did not have my paper finished.
Those papers were embarrassing.
I DID NOT GET ALL THE POINTS.

One day, they had a meeting with me to tell me...

THEY WERE GOING TO KICK ME OUT OF COLLEGE!
I begged them for one more chance.

From then on it looked like this...

THAT'S GENIUS!...

On the day I received the assignment;
I would leave the class go straight to the library and write the paper. I would go back and find the teacher that day and
- ASK THEM TO READ IT
- ASK IF IT WAS A 100% GRADE
- ASK WHAT I NEEDED TO CHANGE OR ADD TO MAKE IT A 100% GRADE.
- I THEN IMMEDIATELY MADE ANY CHANGES AND BROUGHT IT RIGHT BACK TO THEM. The changes only took moments to make, because they told me what I needed to do, but often made up 10% or more of the grade.
- I had stumbled upon a fool proof method.

At first the teachers were thrown off, no one does this!
In fact, most teachers were a little annoyed.
But after the first couple of times they expected it. By the 3rd time they
were so impressed that it quickly changed everyone's perception of me.
I became known as the go-getter!
The teachers wished ALL the students would work so hard!
I NEVER WORRIED ABOUT COMPLETING A PAPER OR WHAT
GRADE I WOULD GET AGAIN. IT HAD TO BE 100%
OR I WOULD JUST CHANGE IT UNTIL IT WAS.
I would finish the paper, check it with the teacher, and KNOW I was
getting my 100%.

THEN
I would take a nap
eat some dinner
and go PLAY!
WITH MORE TIME
WORRY FREE!
AND WITH STRAIGHT A'S!

I went from almost kicked out
to the Dean's list.

Once you try this method you will never go back.

A.C.T.

What is the ACT?

The ACT is a national college admissions examination that consists of subject area tests in:

English   **Mathematics Reading**   **Science**

The ACT Plus Writing includes the four subject area tests plus a 30-minute Writing Test.

ACT results are accepted by all four-year colleges and universities in the U.S.

The ACT includes 215 multiple-choice questions and takes approximately 3 hours and 30 minutes to complete, including a short break (or just over four hours if you are taking the ACT Plus Writing). Actual testing time is 2 hours and 55 minutes (plus 30 minutes if you are taking the ACT Plus Writing).

So...
ITS A
BiG TEST.

This was copied and pasted from ACT.org

Google it...go to FAQ.

Your ACT score is as important or MORE important than your GPA!

- You take the ACT test usually during your Junior and Senior year.

So... WHY WORRY ABOUT MY ACT NOW?

- Colleges accept students and give scholarships based on ACT scores.

- It is better to have a HIGH ACT score and a less than perfect GPA, than vice versa.

- Kids usually take the test, do worse on it than they thought they would, and then scramble to get a higher score.

A friend of mine
worked out a deal with his son, John.

John's Dad said,
"Instead of getting a typical teenage job
and starting the
-work,
so you can have a car,
so you can drive to
work-
vicious cycle...

if you take online practice ACT tests
for one hour every night for an ENTIRE year
before taking the real test,
including figuring out how to answer the
questions you get wrong—
one hour every night, one whole year—
I will buy you a car,
pay your insurance,
and give you some spending money."

MY
PARENTS
WOULD
... NEVER
DO THAT.

John got a perfect score on his ACT test.

He received a FULL RIDE SCHOLARSHIP
to the University of Missouri. I'm
STARTING
To SEE HOW
THIS WORKS.

Mizzou
paid for his tuition, books, dorm, and food.

I have another friend, Christy.
Her daughter, Jill, is a 4.0 student.
Jill took the ACT and got a 28.
This was not good enough for Jill.

Christy hired an ACT coach.

The coach taught Jill **<u>HOW</u>** to take the ACT,

because there are "tricks" to everything.

Jill retook the test.

This time Jill received a **33** on her ACT.

The difference in scholarships between

a 28 and a 33 score IS NIGHT & DAY!

Those 5 points are worth

$$THOUSANDS AND THOUSANDS$$

www.khanacademy.org

Legend has it that Mr. Khan was tutoring his family members over the internet with videos that made math easier to understand.

Ann Doerr, Bill & Melinda Gates, Google, and others came along and funded Mr. Khan's idea.

Now Khan has thousands of tutorial videos on multiple subjects. Cool...

YOU can get on khanacademy.org and learn what you need to learn step by step through incremental video lessons to reach your peak potential on the ACT - VERY Cool... For FREE!

AND you can take practice ACT tests through Khan.

My 7 & 8 year olds have an account and spend time every week on Khan.

They will be ready for the ACT.

Real Life Story…

I was standing at my classroom door when an 8th grader stormed up to me.

"Can I go to the office?" he said in an angry tone.

"Why?" I asked him.

"I want to go tell on the math teacher- she drives me crazy."

"Why?" I asked.

"She makes math so confusing."

"So you want to go to the office and tell on a 15 year veteran math teacher because she makes math confusing? Do you think the office is going to side with you?"

"Well…what do you think I should do?"

"I would buy her a gift card for the holidays. She holds your grade in her hands. Even in math most grades are subjective."

"I'm not worried about my grade; I know how to do the math! I am two lessons ahead of her on khanacademy. I've been doing that since you told us about it at the beginning of the semester. I HAVE to be ahead of her- she makes everything harder than it is!"

"That's great!" I said, "But she still controls your grade. It stinks…but it is reality."

"…maybe your right…" he said, and sat down.

As he walked away I realized this was the future of education…this is how the quiet revolution of young people against "old school" education would happen…"I've already learned the material on-line…what else do you have for me?"

Math

is a beast.

Wouldn't it be cool to know how to do it before class even started?

Try khanacademy·org

PRACTICE THE ACT.

- On khanacademy.org
- Daily, Weekly, Sundays, Something!
- Starting NOW
- There are local classes
- There are coaches
- There are practice and tip books
- There are on-line classes
- There are on-line practice tests
- YOUR ACT SCORE IS WORTH TENS OF THOUSANDS OF DOLLARS.

THE **X**TRA FACTOR

My son's wrestling coach has a favorite story. He tells the kids that he won <u>ZERO</u> matches his first year in wrestling and eventually he earned a <u>HALF RIDE SCHOLARSHIP</u> to <u>OHIO STATE UNIVERSITY!</u>

<u>He wrestled for Ohio State and they paid HALF of his college cost and he NEVER won a single match his first year!</u>

<u>YOU HAVE TO DO SOMETHING "XTRA"!</u>

Colleges are not just interested in GPA's ·
HIGH GPA'S ARE A GIVEN, without them you
stand in line behind the people with them·

With high GPA'S and good ACT scores,
the next question colleges ask is...

"WHAT ELSE YOU GOT KID?"

Colleges like it if you are a cool person·
They look at the XTRA things you have done
besides grades·

So...
IT'S THE
STUFF I DO ...
THAT COLLEGES
LOOK AT TOO?

This is the XTRA FACTOR·

Here is the trick to the "XTRA FACTOR"...

Find a way to

<u>TURN WHAT YOU LOVE TO DO</u>

into your XTRA FACTOR.

- Join a SPORT or CLUB, at school, that you like. Or START ONE!

- Find a company with a career that you are interested in and volunteer to be an intern. Talk to your counselor about tying it back to school.

- START a company! Become a successful young entrepreneur (cutting grass, fixing up old cars, taking photos, selling art, playing in a band, WHATEVER!). Make it an official business. Then volunteer at JA...Junior Achievement. Take photos!!! Tie it back to school, business classes, business club- don't have one- start one- be the president!

- Turn your interest into a Community Service. Be creative about it.

- Put on a skateboard show at a retirement home. Make it a community service project through school.
  You get to skate, the seniors will love it.

- *Play guitar for an Elementary school classroom. Tell a story with it. Go back to your 2nd grade teacher- she will love it.*

- *Didn't make the play? Do a monologue or one act with friends. Go back to your middle school Drama teacher- she will love it.*

- *Document XTRA FACTORS through your school counselor. Take lots of photos and movies.*

I GET IT!
I NEED TO HAVE
A POLISHED PRESENTATION
OF MY DOCUMENTED
SCHOOL PARTICIPATION.

NOW...

OK...

THIS IS THE

LEVERAGE

PART!

LEVERAGE NOW

- TIME

- TEACHER

- PARENT

How?...

TIME Leverage

YOUR GOAL IS NOT ONLY TO GET A
SCHOLARSHIP BY THE END OF HIGH SCHOOL,
IT IS ALSO TO DO IT IN THE MOST
EFFICIENT AND EFFECTIVE
WAY POSSIBLE!

MAXIMIZING YOUR
AMOUNT OF
FREE TIME.
NOW!

TIME...

1. Do your PROJECTS the first day they are assigned.
   That will free up more "in class" time.
2. Use this class time to finish your homework & worksheets ~ AT SCHOOL.
3. You can easily do this because you have read your new chapters the first night after the test, before the teacher starts the new unit, so you know the information and you know right where to find it.
4. If you don't know where an answer is within 2 minutes, ask for help, because you have established the HUMAN FACTOR.
5. You will be READY for the TEST because you read all of the material the first day, which gave you an advantage of hearing and understanding the material for the rest of the unit.
6. You directly asked the teacher what is on the test and in what format.
7. Besides, you have analyzed the last study guide & chapters so you pretty much know what is coming on this test. No need to crash study for hours.

IT'S SO CRAZY, IT JUST MIGHT WORK:

THIS IS A DIFFERENT APPROACH THAN "Just Gettin' By"

IT WILL TAKE A WHILE TO GET GOOD AT IT.

(Another reason to start HEADS UP! during 8th grade)

BUT ONCE YOU DO, SCHOOL WORK WILL GET DONE MUCH FASTER!

YOU WILL HAVE MORE FREE TIME FOR YOU!

TEACHER Leverage

WHEN you are a **"HEADS UP!"** student
and have...

- THE HUMAN FACTOR
- Made it clear you want to do well
- Done all the work
- Talked to the teacher on a regular basis
- Checked in with the teacher about your grades repeatedly
- Established a positive relationship with the teacher

THAT
WOULD
BE
COOL ...

YOU WILL

BE TREATED DIFFERENTLY

BY THE TEACHER.

YOU WILL HAVE MORE TRUST,
FREEDOM, AND FLEXIBILITY IN THE
CLASSROOM.

PARENT Leverage

"Just Gettin' By"

Parent: "Billy did you finish your homework?"
Billy: "I'M GOING TO…SHEESSSh…that's not due until Wednesday…besides now I have a B- in that class and I did have a D so leave me alone…
by the way can I have a new phone, a ride, $20.00, and go to the party?"

Parent: "No."

HEADS UP!

William: "Parents could I please discuss something with you.
I have been trying some new things this semester.
You may have noticed that you have not had to remind me to do my homework.
You will be pleased to know that I am receiving all "A's" this quarter.
(always prove it first- don't give them the ole "I'm gonna").
I have a new plan for school.
That plan is to get every point possible that my teachers offer and therefore get straight "A's".
I plan to continue getting straight "A's" throughout high school and receive a 4.0 cumulative GPA.
I am studying ACT practice test on khanacademy.org 3 times a week.
I have joined the school team.
My goal is to get the maximum scholarship I can to Kick-Hiney University where I hope to attend college."

Parents: "Who are you really?"

William: "I was hoping for some support in the pursuit of this new plan. It would really help me if you could provide me with $25 a week allowance and a car when I turn 16."
(Fill in your reasonable wants and desires here- everyone's financial and home life circumstances are unique.)

Parents: "If you maintain this goal we can agree to $15 a week and you can use the mini-van when you need it."
(They will fill in slightly less than you asked for-they can't help it.)

RUN WITH ANYTHING THEY GIVE YOU!

YOU WILL WANT TO HAVE **HEADS UP!**

WHETHER YOUR PARENTS SUPPORT YOU OR NOT,

THIS IS ABOUT YOU!

When you the student TAKE CHARGE

and positively LEAD your own life

you no longer have to be

PUSHED- PULLED- DIRECTED- YELLED AT- BEGGED OR

THREATENED

BY YOUR PARENTS.

YES!

You are on the 18 side of 10-14-18.

YOU ARE IN CHARGE
because you have taken charge of yourself.

YOUR PARENTS LINE UP BEHIND YOU
IN SUPPORT OF YOU
&
YOUR GOALS AND EFFORTS.

Students tell me that **Parent Leverage**
ends up being one of the best
and most dramatic changes in their lives.

STUDENTS WHO USE **HEADS UP!**
HAVE A NEW AND IMPROVED
RELATIONSHIP WITH THEIR PARENTS.

EVERYONE IS HAPPIER.

Check List

✓ Create a Plan to PAY for college.
- Work with your parents.
- Explore colleges that interest you
- Get *FIRED UP ABOUT IT!*

✓ Decide to get a high **GPA** -every point possible.
- Be cool to teachers-
  - ➢ THE HUMAN FACTOR
- Do ALL the easy work-
  - ➢ EASY POINTS
- Nail the tests & projects-
  - ➢ HARD POINTS

✓ Practice your **ACT** test
- Get on khanacademy.org
- Use practice books
- Get an ACT tutor (a lot of it is knowing HOW to take the test)

✓ Begin the **"XTRA FACTOR"**
- Join a school sports team
- Join or create school clubs
- Do and document service projects

✓ Use your new **"LEVERAGE NOW"**

- Time, Teacher, Parent
- Enjoy being on the 18 side of 10-14-18

Final Thoughts

I believe it is only fair that you understand the

"rules" in the game you are playing.

This book has shown some tricks on how to work the school system for potentially better college entry and scholarships.

I hope you are inspired and have good luck.

Having a high GPA, ACT and great Xtra Factor will give you much better options at the end of high school.

And having part, most, or all of your college paid for will give you even more options as a young adult.

On one hand it is all about the money

but I also hope you use those improved options to remember...

The real gift of being a human being is using your insatiable curiosity, ability to create, & love of learning

toward the continuous improvement of

life for all people on spaceship earth.

KIND OF HEAVY DUDE.

I know but it had to be said.

Heads Up 8th Grader!

The End

or really...

THE

BEGINNING!

Now I KNOW HOW IT WORKS! ...THE REST IS UP TO ME.

46436511R00052

Made in the USA
San Bernardino, CA
06 March 2017